Wolf in the Suitcase

poems by

D. Dina Friedman

Finishing Line Press
Georgetown, Kentucky

Wolf in the Suitcase

Copyright © 2019 by D. Dina Friedman
ISBN 978-1-63534-858-3 First Edition
All rights reserved under International and Pan-American Copyright Conventions. No part of this book may be reproduced in any manner whatsoever without written permission from the publisher, except in the case of brief quotations embodied in critical articles and reviews.

ACKNOWLEDGMENTS

The following poems have been previously published:

"Blue" and "Isaac at the Temple Mount" in *New Plains Review*
"Bridge" in *Negative Capability*
"Forgiveness" in *Damfino Journal*
"Hidden Child" in *America Is Not the World*—Pankhearst Press,
       and in *Sow's Ear Review*
"Letter to God from Florida" in *Cargo*
"Munich" and "Ruins" in *Bloodroot*
"Narcissus on the Road" in *Bluestem*
"Salad" in *Midway Journal*
"Seven Lessons Learned from Sea Turtles" in *Mount Hope*
"Waiting" in *Oyez Review*
"Where I Am From" in *Red Booth Review*
"Wolf in the Suitcase" in *Common Ground Review*

Many thanks:
To M. Yoshi for the cover art: http://artbyyoshi.com
To Michael Hirtle for the author photo

Publisher: Leah Maines
Editor: Christen Kincaid
Cover Art: M. Yoshi, http://artbyyoshi.com
Author Photo: Michael Hirtle
Cover Design: Leah Huete

Printed in the USA on acid-free paper.
Order online: www.finishinglinepress.com
        also available on amazon.com

Author inquiries and mail orders:
Finishing Line Press
P. O. Box 1626
Georgetown, Kentucky 40324
U. S. A.

Table of Contents

Wolf in the Suitcase 1

Where I Am From 2

Narcissus on the Road 3

Waiting 4

Bridge 5

T'fillin 6

Cage 8

We Are Stuck in October 10

Munich 12

I and It 14

The Tenth Plague 16

Salad 18

Isaac at the Temple Mount: 2014 19

Hidden Child 20

Ruins 22

Blue 23

Forgiveness 24

Letter to God from Florida 25

Seven Lessons Learned from Sea Turtles 26

*For my daughter, Alana,
in admiration of her passion, persistence, and palate*

WOLF IN THE SUITCASE

Carted back, to my baby house,
it bounded—breaking lamps
and brittle things, darkening

what had already dimmed:
wolf in the unspoken
wolf in the thick air

wolf in all I do not dare
to say, biting at the zippered close;
the suitcase does its blinded,

muzzled dance, bludgeons through hallways
down brick steps where begonias bloom
in the blighted yard. It's crying,

"Touch me not."
It claims it can see in the dark.

WHERE I AM FROM

I am from buildings and concrete, from subways lined with spit,
thick letters announcing untaken exits.

I am from dirt, the dying sand under backyard sidewalks,
where carrot tops killed for space in the one available crack.

I am from weeds, and the miracle of bulbs
returning to their place of birth. I am from ink, spilling and spilt,

then bursting veins, like businessmen swarming out of subways.
I am from dinner parties and dirty plates,

from the shades pulled in the living room,
where Great-Grandma sat in her black chair peeking out

between soiled Venetian blinds as I emerged
in a starched skirt twirling under its own steam

like a 50s dream.

NARCISSUS ON THE ROAD

Admit it, you might be driving through North Dakota
imagining the movie you'd make, if that movie was your life:
a string of Oscar moments, where you actually kissed
the crushes of your adolescent days, sent the suicide notes

composed in your mind, running the camera on close up
to see their faces as they read your desperation. Did they really love you
or was it all montage? Fantasy trips to Paris: pillows, and fade to black;
your funeral with the volume turned up, the camera igniting

the glow of your reflection as they sob and say beautiful things.
It's all about unleashing your inner plot,
driving recklessly down the highway, which is lined with sunflowers
and bland as toast. Your life, the perfect tragi-comedy,

as the cop pulls you over, close to the Montana border,
and you imagine the non-family-friendly version of the movie
as they clip on the cuffs. It might be the best thing that's ever happened:
a concoction of get-aways, thriller chase scenes,

a clock ticking toward the death you can't escape from
even if you never had the intention of ending your life
a second earlier than fate intended.
Ah, fate! If only you'd already divined the end.

WAITING

There's energy when stories wait for endings:
doomed romance, a growing tumor,
a loved one gone crazy with an axe. The imagination soars

but the dog waits for ordinary things
a walk in the woods, samples from breakfast.
The cat, who does not believe in waiting,
lies like an elegant sculpture on the Guatemalan blanket,
the one we first tried to get in that small town
two hours away on the chicken bus.

We had to wait to tell the story,
how strangers sat so close to us
they could have been in our laps, how you could see spots
where their teeth were missing, smell their lunches,

and when we got to the town, there were no blankets,
because it wasn't the day for market.
Instead, there were stores that sold plastic things,
and a town square painted pink, where people lounged.
Perhaps they were waiting, though I don't know why, or for what.

I have a snapshot of that square, and today is also a snapshot.
Stagnant. All this waiting settles like fog.
Even when the endings aren't pretty, it's hard to resist temptation,
press fast forward, feel the brunt of the denouement,
imagine the place where the stories end.

BRIDGE

My parents never crossed The Kissing Bridge.
I sat behind them in the stagnant heat.
They swerved away, sweat trickling
down their necks. I caught a flash

of lovers spread on stones, a whirl
of tongues and skin. The car approaching honked.
The sky blushed pink, then faded into dark.
We headed home. No stars, no moon.

How would they find their way
when they were done? Or would they spend the night
out in the fog? When love was false,
the bridge suspension swung,

the legend said. I didn't care.
I swore, one night I'd sneak out of my room
and curve into a body hot as stars.

T'FILLIN

My kid, corralled by the corner *Hasid*
poses bound on the streets of T'sfat

straps of *t'fillin* buckling blue hair.
"It's your *bar mitzvah!*"

The man Heavens his arms, intones the *Sh'ma,*
prayer to be echoed, one word at a time,

like one God. Illusion of unity
in this dotty country, each corner a contradiction

in coverings: the modest shielding *shvitzing* skin,
heathen tourists in shorts

clicking cameras for future Facebook froth.
I anticipate the caption: "Look at me,

with my *T'fillin!*" Hooked
under the man's arm, my sheepish second-born

smirks behind sunglasses,
unravels the leather straps

as soon as the camera snaps, eager to leave
for countries once locked behind the Iron Curtain.

The man extends his palm, a final supplication.
"I performed your *bar mitzvah!*"

he shouts, fists raised to the faceless clouds
as we leave his hand empty, slink down alleys

toward galleries, and the local cheese.
My child never posts the picture.

No shots until Georgia: a man balanced on scaffolding
repairing lattice in an ancient synagogue gallery.

so close to where my great-great grandmother
once crossed herself when the Cossacks came,

claimed, "Christians live here."
A vital lie to save her unbound body.

CAGE
(after Martha Ronk: Greek phrenitikos, frantic)

Republican children   are just like ours

restless   underneath and underneath

somewhere blood   a heart   somewhere

playing on swing-sets   somewhere squirming in church.

Immigrant children   are just like ours

somewhere   underneath and underneath

scrunched space blankets   restless   wondering

where are their mothers   somewhere

eaten by wolves.   Or had the gangs come?

Silence is molasses.   Words stick

even when their parents manage to call.

Somewhere a bug crawls   on the chain link fence

that isn't a cage   no more than a church is a cage

when the doors are closed.   And our children

are just like theirs   restless   underneath and underneath

a blond boy squirms   against his mother's grip.

He wants to be wild   on a swing-set somewhere

not this cage of a room   wedged in by parents

holding pictures of children   in cages

children like Pablito   cowering   somewhere

a man with jowls   barks strange sounds

que no entienden.   *Es el Diablo.*   Our blond boy knows

this building with the wolf men

has some connection   to the children   taken

underneath and underneath   their parents' grips.

Will they come for me?   Silence is molasses.

The wolves might be listening.   Though everyone's yelling

with their outside voices   words about cages.   He wishes

like Pablito   *que no entiende.*   He wishes

he were swinging   so high   the chains would creak.

His mommy grips harder   her hand is a cage.   Somewhere

there are wolves   restless

underneath and underneath   somewhere

blood   a heart   somewhere

an urge to run.

WE ARE STUCK IN OCTOBER
(after John Ashbery: The Chateau Hardware)

It's raining again, and the remnants of leaves
shellacked on the slippery stoop test our dogged
tenacity. It's a dead time.

Trees choke red while people laugh
and point, lingering, the way one does
at funerals, unable to leave the show-horse

body, its lips like plastic fruit.
Remember how Uncle M. would eat
those phony grapes to make us laugh?

When he lay there embalmed, I thought of him splayed
in the armchair, watching the Yankees deflate,
no longer Bronx bombers in the bombed out Bronx.

You said he wasn't much different in death.
He never talked that much. Once
we went to see the Yankees, before

athletes took knees at the national anthem
to protest quick-triggered police, before
the fallen leaves were slick, and we had

to beware of our balance. Don't trust the beauty
of changing colors. The days are shorter,
darker. This weather is kind of a jail.

Yesterday, I heard the geese exulting
escape, sirens of honks and truth,
as if they knew hurricanes, wildfires, rising

water. A car alarm bleated a clashing,
distant pitch. No one paid
attention to the warning. Like stadium cries

for hot dogs, beer, we blot them out:
too normal in these slippery, tilted times.

MUNICH

In pictures I leaned my olive cheek
against your Aryan face

trying to cross the veiled space
between us, elusive as your ash-blond head

tall enough to dare the sky.
Always, I tried not to cry,

tried to smile and beguile.
I sat on your lap like a child

a dark doll, with curly hair.
We made such an odd-looking pair.

I was heavier then.
Hansel's witch could have pushed me in the oven;

your hot passion
charmed my lips to your chest,

smooth as a girl's but broad
like a flank of meat.

I had a coat made out of a sheep
dyed green. The more you hated it,

the more I wore it, but it was no consolation
for the wolf I should have been

when they stopped me for alien.
Demanding my papers, they left you free,

just as you left me,
a stray moth hovering above the wires,

as I stood where fires consumed my ancestors' hair.
We were an impossible pair.

I carried the stories with me:
the pianist's sour whisper

when my grandfather, alone in Germany,
played for the violin master.

Her words, "dirty Jew," incessant as fugue,
echo oceans and years away

and when the war started, he couldn't play,
insisted the music held messages,

code to cart bodies away.
He had to quit the symphony

and think about fish
thriving in their own universe

thousands of feet below.
I cannot go

with you
to see the glockenspiel,

neat and timed,
primed to chime

a signal to forget,
to move on, without regret.

I AND IT

Twirling by the mirror, my skirt powder blue,
I knew I was a Jew. It was in the book
with armies on the cover—Bible stories

read hovered in the shabby Hebrew
school by the airport runway, where I whirled
wild in the bathroom, a dervish at the mirror.

Other people look like people,
but I don't look human.
Not a real person. This

is my body? This is my blood? What
is solid? Thoughts are air, but thoughts
are the anchor: the rock, the talk, the need

for God, a breath of wind and rules
who looks like no one we can see.
Thank you, God, but I prefer

the tree of knowledge over trust.
And I admit to blasphemy,
even if I don't exist

outside my thoughts. But you, God, need
my thoughts to frame your form.
Unification. Isn't that what we're up

against? My hair, defining my difference,
curled and out of control. The sprinkled
Yiddish from the ancestors' lair, where dragons

guard the *klezmer* chords, links
to 300 original *Ashkenazis*
from whom we've supposedly sprung. Who cares

about Sephardic Ungreat-Great-
Great-Great… Grandpa De Leon,
who may be fake or a conquistador?

Better to claim potato peasants
raped by Cossacks; girl in blue
whose face doesn't look like a face, your face.

Everyone else is real. But I?
This form? I live in my thoughts, willows
or clouds, or something else that fleets

and slips. A bird. A duck. A piece
of dust. Didn't the Bible say
we're dust? Why don't they trust us?

Why does the girl twirl? Why won't she unfurl?
And why tame that curl? Stop. And fall
in love with the tree. Stop

and fall in love with the body.

THE TENTH PLAGUE

> *"I shall go out in the midst of Egypt. Every firstborn in the land of Egypt shall die, from the first born of the Pharaoh who sits on his throne to the first born of the maidservant who is behind the millstone and all the first born of beast." Exodus 11: 5-6*

I didn't choose to be born here—it was time to reincarnate
and we didn't have maps. I couldn't point
to preferred places, or know the sketchy spots, like Egypt
in the time people believed in statues,

except those Jews and their burning-bush God,
the one who liked to play pranks with frogs
and change the color of rivers. We locals didn't take it seriously.
We'd seen locusts before. Too many would make any cow go crazy.

But this last rampage …the court should have had The Guy
by the balls. It was one of those random jobs,
targeting anyone born before his brothers.
I wouldn't kill a lamb to save myself.

I thought I could mark my door with the bloody river,
but it was too dilute. Like I said, I had no choice.
No one did. The Guy had hardened the Pharaoh's heart,
It was a mind-game, plague-like illusion of free will.

We were pulled putty in his hands, doomed by accident
of birth. I'd lived too good a former life to be reborn as ant.
Only insects were immune; too many eggs
to figure which hatched first. He even included mammals

as if a cat could carry an Egyptian passport
and bear responsibility for the sins of some king
it could care less about. I was just a shepherd.
What did I know of Pharaohs? What justice here?

Tzedek, tzedek, tirdof! Next year in Jerusalem,
they say, or forty more in the celestial desert
before being reborn as lawyer, activist, savior,
messenger of justice speaking into megaphones

madly litigating against the clock:
statutes of limitation on unprosecuted crimes.

SALAD
(Orlando, June 12, 2016)

It's a vegan grief binge:
a whole head of lettuce
dismembered leaves

bodies strewn under disco lights.
What music was playing?
ED? Indie? Whimsy?

Nothing whimsical about this day
chopping cucumbers and carrots;
adding almonds for protein, mint

for the taste of tears. Across the field,
cows yawn in the barn, lazy
as they approach the robot milkers.

The sun glows hot, parching the sad squash.
I make a note to spot-water at dusk, too lazy
to drag the hose. The bouncer braved the spray,

wrenched the secret door, led the lucky
like Moses seeking a promised land. His name: Imran Yousef.
The papers don't state his religion, or if he needed one.

Only the gunman's—important as his preference
for salad dressing: Blue Cheese?
Green Goddess? A preacher asks

if we can truly be sad
about murdering Sodomites.
The sun shines over the kale,

and the cilantro stretching away from its roots.
All part of the salad—needy, and seeking harvest.
Soon. Before everything bolts.

ISAAC AT THE TEMPLE MOUNT: 2014

You might obey the sign, forbidding entry
to holy ground, or follow your delusional father,
who mutters to the sky. You might carry
firewood for offerings, or take pictures
of the mosque: the cool blue tile, the golden dome.
You might wear a ring in your brow, or dye
your hair green. You might hum along
with the *muezzin*, as you remember
your cast-off brother, the miracle of wells that saved him
from your mother's jealousy. You might believe
your father was a fool when he pulled his knife,
told you to listen to the illusion of breath
emanating high from clouds as it traveled down
to this rocky summit, where soldiers now survey
the praying shoeless men, prostrate and facing east
in the sluggish air that smells like seared sheep. You might
wish you'd already learned to play the harp
or speak your mind, aspirations that have always been
on the list of things to do before you die.

HIDDEN CHILD

My parents fled from me,
leaving only ghosts, their long legs thwarted

at the Swiss-German border. No songbursts
on snow-covered Alps. No flowered meadows,

only the brown boot of the brown shirt
pounding down on my mother's cheek.

I imagine the sound of her neck
breaking, like the neck of a bird

and try to find her blurred face
in mine. I've been told I look like a bird,

my nose a beak, my neck too long
for my old and egg-shaped head.

Now in the Promised Land,
I watch great birds fly to the carob tree

where Bar Yochai, ancient sage of the *Kabbalah*,
ate while he hid for twelve years

in the cave whose mouth opens
in my garden. Why did life bring me here

if not to highlight the legacy of hiding?
When teens with torches surrounded our home,

putting on their show of Jew-hating
we had to leave our chickens, our flowering trees.

The neighbors watched the holy cave,
though no one came to pray. Like my life, the hole, empty.

There are times I need dark rooms.
And other times, chickens, a warm egg in my hand.

RUINS
> *"The day is a woman who loves you."*
> —Richard Hugo

It might be a Sunday.
You might turn to her on a whim
because her skin reminds you of the desert.

You could drink her mouth.
It's the only water around
or nestle in bristles of cactus you once called hair

or sit together in the pews,
like a couple that has known each other too long,
without realizing the church has been deserted

due to issues of liability. But you could take that risk.
Perhaps, if you stroke your beard, it might whiten back
to the time of Moses. Now it's red, stained

with sins you can only think about committing.
There's no name for them. Just as there's no name for this day,
or this kiva, where the ancients prayed

and you have decided to sit,
a sliver of moon shining on the lone ladder out.
Three of the rungs are missing.

BLUE

Forgive your orange doubt, its shellacked peel.
Believe in blue and be cool. Jump

into the blue pool, a blue that doesn't bind, or blind.
Blue kiss. Blue death. A blue win—or sin.

Mean blues, obscene blues.
Put on your midnight shoes
and dance, schmooze; embrace the slide
of the sobbing guitar, the high arcing dive,

dark blue gasp on the prickly horizon. My baby left me
and you have left your babyhood,
the smiling orange juice mother who wiped your eyes,
the cliché of blue skies,
settling like our worn blanket song,

We seek comfort in the little we know.
Jump into the blue water and go.

FORGIVENESS

Leaping out of the lake, you emerge as elephant
playing blues, trunk thumping over your mother's twelve bars:
tonic to dominant and back. You'd add the seventh,
if you knew she'd forgive you, if it didn't taste like salt.
Instead you sink into the groove, channel Ray Charles
hiding behind those glasses. It's safer that way,
but you forgive him, forgive yourself, because it's in the directions,
even if the dog scarfed up the bread you dribbled
into *Rosh Hashanah* waters, symbolic crumbs
from those gloopy New-Age days.
Holding hands with people you wished you liked better,
you chanted the scripted prayers, easier if you ignored translation,
relied on the elephant's chords. God loves us
because she has no other choice, the way you love your children,
or your mother, even when they piss you off. *Gornischt Helfin.*
Your thin scarf of devotion is losing its threads.
It tastes like Lot's Wife, who couldn't leave doubt behind.
Faith is hot, like *vindaloo*. It makes the heart spasm, the mouth sweat.
You could jump into a lake of it, but blues are the only forgiveness
to dive for. Even an elephant will tell you that,
and so will the piano, those same twelve bars,
the old men *davening*, droning, drilling their metal chant
until you have no choice but to pick up the piano
and heave it with divine strength
into the frothing water, the first act
for which you'll truly need to be forgiven.

LETTER TO GOD FROM FLORIDA

Thank you for the crab scuttling to the ocean's edge, for creating edges
and the concept of edgy; for days without the happy magenta hue

of the F train and the people on the platform playing Angry Birds.
Thank you for pelicans and the electronic New York Times,

antidote to neighbors' newsprint flapping in our faces. Thank you
for pouches, speedos, bikinis baring our skin to the balmy air;

for atheism and words without the letter "e," and for Scrabble,
especially the "z," for orchestras and rabbits

but next time get the brass in tune, for the moon
goddess's dictate to kow-tow; thanks a lot for our daily chow, for alligators,

and those microscopic nits I picked for days
out of my daughter's hair. Seriously,

thank you for the concept of infinity;
and this nitty vacation sand, shifting hot

as I dig my elbows down, raise my sacred torso,
stand to face the foam.

SEVEN LESSONS LEARNED FROM SEA TURTLES

I.
The micromanaging mother is unnecessary.
It's enough to lay eggs in the sand
and trust the earth to hatch them.

II.
Keep walking. The sand will forgive indentation.
Eventually the ocean will pull you in.

III.
You can pretend to be a rock.
If you're lucky, no one will notice.
If not, bite.

IV.
The decoy nest, like the decoy word
fools only those who don't look deep.

V.
Learn to see in the dark.
Better yet, learn to compensate
for not being able to see in the dark.

VI.
Rejoice in your long life,
the slow steps of your aging.

VII.
Return to the places you love
even if you're not sure why you love them.

D. Dina Friedman grew up in New York City, a place she still holds close to her heart. She met her husband, Shel Horowitz, forty years ago at an open poetry reading in a fifth-floor walk-up in Greenwich Village. Three years later they moved to western Massachusetts, where they raised their two children, Alana and Rafael, because it was "a compromise between Brooklyn and the Ozarks." She currently lives next door to a farm with 500 cows.

Dina was nominated twice for a Pushcart Prize and has published widely in literary journals including *Calyx, Common Ground Review, Lilith, Pinyon, Negative Capability, New Plains Review, Steam Ticket, Bloodroot, Inkwell, Pacific Poetry and Fiction Review, Tsunami, The Sun, Jewish Currents, Anderbo, San Pedro River Review, Mount Hope,* and *Rhino*. She is also the author of two young adult novels: *Escaping Into the Night* (Simon and Schuster) an Association of Jewish Libraries Notable Book for Older Readers and an American Library Association Best Books for Young Adults nominee; and *Playing Dad's Song* (Farrar Straus Giroux) a Bank Street College of Education Best Book.

Dina received her MFA from Lesley University and teaches at the University of Massachusetts/Amherst. While writing and teaching are central aspects of her life, equally important is working for a better world. A committed activist, Dina has spent many, many hours working on social justice and environmental issues.

When she's not writing, teaching, or doing political work, Dina loves hiking, bicycling, gardening, and traveling. A fun fact about Dina: in addition to visiting more than 30 countries, she's been to all 50 U.S. states.

To learn more about Dina, visit http://www.ddinafriedman.com

CPSIA information can be obtained
at www.ICGtesting.com
Printed in the USA
BVHW030306160319
542849BV00001B/26/P